Part of the
Expand the Possible
series of books

A comprehensive guide
to **vertical development**

PETER BLUCKERT

Published by Peter Bluckert.

www.peterbluckert.com

Copyright © Peter Bluckert 2019

First Published 2019.

ISBN 978-1-9161300-0-5

Typeset and illustrated by Adam Thorp

1.
An introduction to adult development theory

- Introduction and overview
- Stages of development
- Lines of development

Introduction

In this opening chapter, my intention is to provide a solid, reliable introduction to the field of adult development theory which essentially describes how adults develop more comprehensive and complex ways of making sense of themselves and their experience. You may have a reaction to some of the terminology – I certainly do. In fact, many times I've wished that I could have entered the room on a magic carpet and say to the researchers, "No, don't call it that – you will put people off. Find better, simpler words". Alas, no magic carpet, and they had their reasons, so we have what we have. But don't let the terminology obstruct your view. Keep in mind that what's most important are the meanings explained below the definitions. There is some very significant thinking in here.

Overview

Adult development theory has been described variously as evolutionary theory, constructive-developmental psychology, stage development theory, integral theory, and within the leadership context, leadership maturity theory. There are several 'schools' of thinking each with their own frameworks, models and language, sharing a high degree of consensus around the core concepts and propositions. Adult human development has been researched from several different lenses – one of the earliest and best known, Maslow, looked at how needs evolve from basic physical survival and safety through to fulfilment of potential which he called self-actualisation. His hierarchy of needs framework is still taught in many psychology departments and business schools throughout the world. Other researchers, regarded within the adult development field as thought-leaders, have focused on values (Graves, Beck and Cowan), identity (Loevinger), moral development and ethics (Kohlberg), ego maturity (Cook-Greuter), meaning-making (Kegan), and action logics (Torbert).

Each has identified patterns of meaning-making that human beings share in common which are referred to as stages or levels of development. Developmental movement from one stage (level) to the next is often driven by a felt sense of limitations in the current way of constructing meaning and making sense of everyday life; this can happen when a person faces increased complexity in their work or home environment that requires a more comprehensive way of understanding themselves, others and the world.

One of the core propositions of all the various schools of thinking is that people's stage of development influences what they notice or can become aware of, and therefore, what they pay attention to, prioritise and act on. This profound notion has wide-ranging implications, which will become clear as we go deeper into the material.

Interestingly, despite the fact that these schools (of thinking) are long established and robust, many of the core ideas and leading researchers mentioned here are still not widely known - although this is beginning to change. Stage theory is gaining increasing prominence in the adult education, leadership development and coaching fields. Nonetheless, it still has a long way to go before being embraced as mainstream.

Amongst those who are familiar with the theory and practice it would be true to say that it divides opinion. Some people object to the labels whilst others perceive the frameworks as hierarchical, or even elitist, and are concerned that it may suggest a better-worse paradigm of human functioning. Developmental psychologists counter this by saying there is nothing inherently better about later stages of adult development. The critical point is whether there is a good-enough fit between the individual's stage of development and the complexity of the challenges they face into, both in their work and wider lives. The same question applies at the collective level: does an executive team or political leadership's capacity match what they're dealing with?

Unsurprisingly, there are a growing number of observers who believe that we (sapiens) are falling behind the pace and complexity of change and we are already 'in over our heads' with the 'wicked problems' of our time. Both at the individual and collective levels, we need to accelerate our evolutionary growth and development.

To gain a better appreciation of the adult development field, it's important to grasp what's meant by stages (or levels) of development, and lines of development. This is our next stop.

Stages of development

"We do not see things as they are. We see things as we are" - from the Talmud, though often ascribed to Anais Nin.

- One of the important areas of agreement amongst different researchers is that human beings during the course of their lifetime, and humanity over the course of history, evolves in stages. The stages of child development have long since been mapped by Piaget (1954) and others, but in this chapter, I will only be referring to adult development stages.

- Different researchers and adult development schools vary in the number of stages they identify. Many define seven, some confine their framework to four, and others suggest as many as nine (see Developmental frameworks − a map of the territory, later).

- Every stage includes, transcends and builds on the previous. We don't move on and leave ourselves behind. What we have, we keep; who we are, travels with us, nested within us. The image of Russian dolls may be useful here.

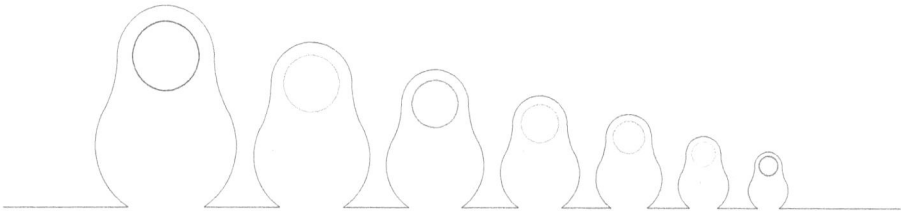

- Given earlier selves are part of us, we continue to have the ability to perceive and operate from previous stages. Sometimes this can be helpful when the context calls for it. Other times, less so, especially when our current situation triggers us to act inappropriately from an earlier stage of maturity. The triggering may be a re-stimulation of unresolved issues (unfinished business) that we've also carried forward.

- We can also find ourselves operating at our higher-self for periods of time, albeit these are likely to be temporary interludes unless we're in transition between stages. These higher-self experiences provide us with glimpses of where we could be and perhaps where we want to be. Sometimes they result from uplift experiences when we experience an unusually high level of personal support and skilled help – such as a personal growth workshop.

- Each stage with its different worldview (mindset or frame of reference) is more comprehensive and effective in dealing with the challenges and complexities of life than its predecessors.

- A person who has reached a later stage can understand earlier worldviews - this capacity to understand is nested as an integrated part of self. In contrast, a person at an earlier stage may not be able to understand the mindset and worldview of stages of development beyond their own – and can't operate from them. They can talk the talk, but they can't walk the walk.

- Stages of development can be accelerated but cannot be skipped. We can't leap-frog a stage.

- Developmental theorists generally divide the spectrum of human development into four tiers: Preconventional, Conventional, Postconventional and Transpersonal, Cook-Greuter (2013). Around 80-85% of the general adult population function within the first two tiers of development, with around 15-20% operating at the later tiers. More detailed explanation of these terms is provided later.

- Until recently the view of many developmental researchers is that we mostly live at our developmental centre of gravity. This is our default, go-to place, although we often resort to behaviour patterns from earlier stages when we're over-extended, stressed or struggling with illness.

- Profiling tools and processes have been available for some time and many of the different schools have developed their own version, claiming a high degree of accuracy in identifying an individual's centre of gravity. In recent years these instruments have become more widely used within the leadership development field. A number of large-scale research studies of organisational managers and leaders have been undertaken.

- At this point in time there seems to be a growing tendency, based on these research findings, to widen the focus from a single centre of gravity to a tri-stage perspective. This means we all have that place in the middle, our centre of gravity, but can also find ourselves operating at one stage higher and one stage lower. Those people who are in transition between stages, and there are many, will often notice the shift between their different worlds. To help you make more sense of this tri-stage notion it may be useful if you ask yourself these questions ... What experiences have you had of yourself at a higher level of consciousness and purpose? And, what experiences have you had of yourself when it's as if you've fallen back? You may want to try to identify the circumstances and key factors in play in both scenarios.

- What you are able to see is different at different stages of development – the world literally looks like a different place. Outside reality hasn't changed; but your interior experience of it, has.

- Your level of consciousness is something you look through, not at. This is why the metaphor of lens is used so often in this theory.

- As you grow and develop, what's important, what interests and concerns you, and what motivates you, tends to change. This can be interesting and exciting when you quickly find the next thing or your new purpose, but can also be disturbing because it will invariably mean letting go of something that has felt important to you - without necessarily knowing what's coming next. And it usually feels risky.

- Growth and development can sometimes be disruptive to your relationships if your loved ones and colleagues are not growing at the same pace, or simply cannot understand your restlessness and need to step again into the unknown. The fear of disrupting core relationships is a common reason why people don't search out development.

- A feature of the earlier stages of development is a strong 'I' perspective and an equally strong sense of rightness – a belief that one's own truth and reality is the correct one, even the only one. Individuals operating from later stages can see the value and importance of these beliefs, understandings and perspectives, but view them as at best, partial. After all, there is no absolute truth, it's all relative. Or is it? Are there some absolutes, some universal truths? Is there something we can call reality? These very questions take on a different complexion at later stages of adult maturity.

- At its core, development theory describes the unfolding of human potential towards deeper understanding, wisdom and effectiveness in the world.

Lines of development

In addition to developmental stages, a series of developmental lines, or multiple intelligences, move through these stages such as cognitive and emotional intelligence, moral and spiritual intelligence and others. These give us our breadth and depth. However, it's important to recognise that we don't necessarily grow at the same pace across them. Typically, there is uneven development across the different lines with some stronger than others. A simple example of this would be the exceptionally bright and intellectually able person who displays low emotional intelligence and relational maturity.

We might assume that people at higher levels of cognition (intellect) would score at least at medium or even at high on the ethics and values line. Life experience tells us, of course, that this is not necessarily the case.

There can be some fairly obvious reasons why some lines might be strongly developed, others moderately, and some poorly developed. Different lines need to be more strongly developed for different kinds of work and role. For example, a team leadership role where success can only be achieved through creating a resonant culture with high collaboration and trust will tend to provide more scope for developing behavioural and personal impact skills than an individual contributor expert role where the person works primarily on their own. And if those lines aren't deemed strong enough, the team leader will certainly get to know about it. Whereas, the individual contributor may be tolerated if they're delivering the results in their own area.

Sometimes an individual with strong lines of development finds themselves in roles where they can't make use of them due to the nature of their roles. For example, they may have strong emotional connection and sensibilities but find themselves staring at a computer screen for most of the day analysing data. This might grow their cognitive line, albeit marginally, but other parts of them are lying fallow. Researchers hold different positions on how many lines of development or multiple intelligences exist.

Lines of Development

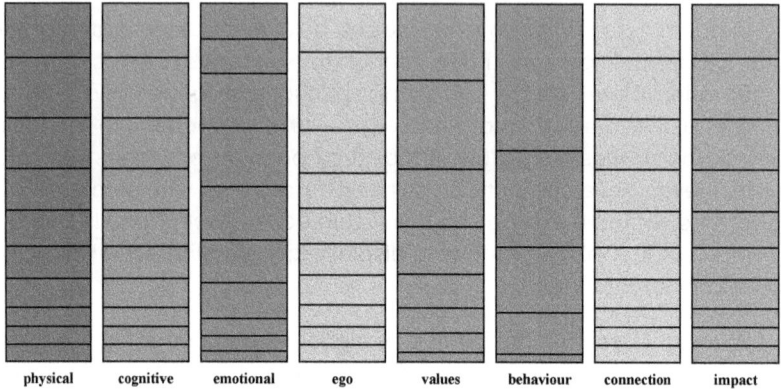

Vertical Development

| physical | cognitive | emotional | ego | values | behaviour | connection | impact |

Source: Watkins (2015)

This list of 'eight most commercially relevant lines of development for most businesses' offered by Watkins (2014), closely approximates to the majority view. There is a notable absence - the spiritual line. Authors and organisational consultants seeking credibility and executive access within the corporate world can take a pragmatic view on discussing spirituality. They don't believe it will be well received so avoid it. Whilst this is true in many executive suites, my own experience is that privately many are looking to have this conversation. For some people, it's not simply part of their lives; it's at the core of their lives. I don't include it here in my adapted version because I share Benner's view (2012) that spiritual development is not well represented as one amongst many lines of development, but rather as 'primary and foundational to all'.

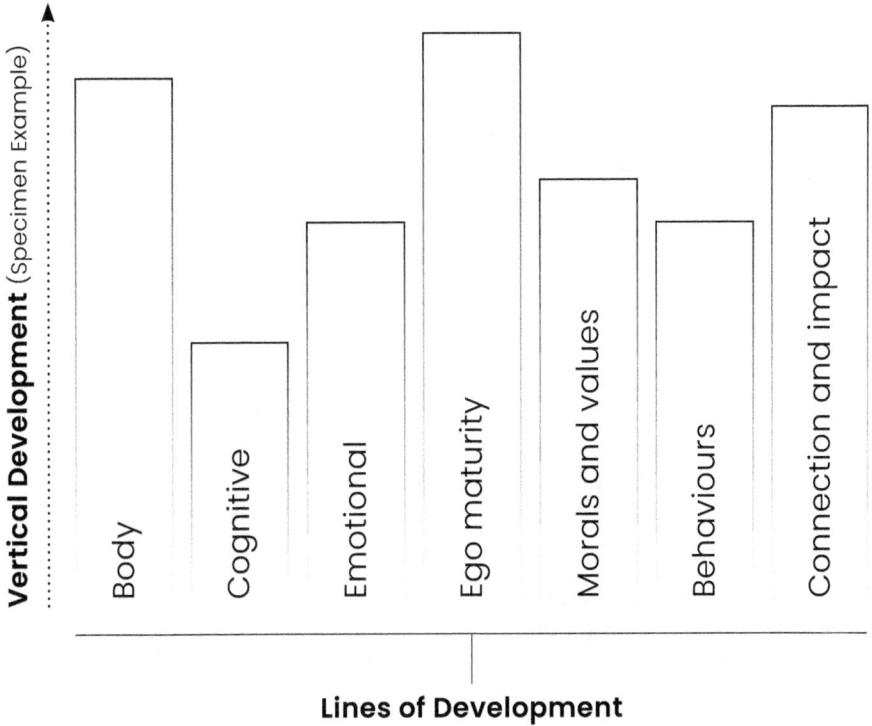

Lines of Development

The lines of development are presented here as separate. And they can be developed independently. People go to the Gym, Yoga or Pilates to develop their physical (body) line. They read books and go on educational programmes to develop their cognitive line.

However, it's important to recognise that these lines inter-connect in profound ways. In the case of Yoga and Pilates, people often experience growth across other lines such as the spiritual and emotional. Cognitive learning can raise awareness across all the lines.

Powerful combinations

Combinations which have great significance, both in the leadership space and in wider life, are emotional development and ego maturity. When we see progress in the emotional line, a higher level of emotional intelligence, combined with more advanced ego development, this shows up in more mature behaviours. In the relational space, this alters the nature of connection and impact. And when leaders operate from a considered, principled set of values this can produce a much-needed improvement in ethical behaviours which will often mirror a move from 'me' (ego-centric) to 'us' (group-centric) to 'all of us' (world-centric), Wilber et al (2008).

Ego development

Having introduced many executives and senior leadership teams to these lines of development it's been interesting to observe how often they have gravitated towards one in particular – the ego development line. Regularly asked questions have included, 'Does this mean to have less ego, a less overblown ego?', or, 'is this about having your ego more in control?

Even without any psychological background or training, they've sensed that this is what some have called the 'master trait'. They've quickly seen that as people evolve and transform to later stages of human development, this mysterious and important notion of maturity and possibly wisdom, follows in its wake. For readers who are seeking more technical meaning of ego development, here are some definitions:

'What changes in ego development is an interwoven fabric of impulse control, character, interpersonal relations, conscious preoccupations, and cognitive complexity', Loevinger (1976). In Cook-Greuter's (2000) ego maturity framework, 'a person's ego stage is, by definition, 'that view of reality that he or she most routinely uses to deal with experience'. She also refers to the function of the ego as trying to explain the experiences of our lives, our organising process "the incessant story-teller", the essential meaning-maker. As one matures, the ego tells a new story about who 'I am', and how 'reality works'.

2.
Developmental frameworks and stage definitions – a map of the territory

- Kegan's key concepts and terminology

- Ego maturity and action logics definitions

- Stage transition issues

- Tension points arising out of different worldviews

- Developmental frameworks – a map of the territory

Kegan's key concepts and terminology

Harvard professor and long-time constructive-developmental researcher, Robert Kegan, is an acknowledged authority in this field and one of those at the forefront of stage development theory. His contention is that vertical development catalyses a quantum expansion in mental complexity improving a leader's capability to not only deal better themselves with today's more uncertain, complex, rapidly changing contexts, but also facilitate the cascade of the new capacities throughout their organisations.

Some of Kegan's key concepts have been summarised by his colleague and associate, Jennifer Garvey-Berger who also reproduced them as an Appendix in her book, 'Changing on the Job' (2012).

Constructive developmental psychology

Constructivists believe that the world isn't out there to be discovered, but that we create our world by our discovery of it. Humans make meaning of their surroundings (including their relationships), and that meaning is the surrounding; two people who see the same picture differently may actually, in their seeing of it, be creating two different pictures.

Developmentalists believe that humans grow and change over time and enter qualitatively different phases of increasing complexity as they grow.

Subject-Object theory

Subject-Object theory is a constructive-developmental approach to understanding human experience and how we construct meaning. For Kegan, and for many other developmental psychologists, the changing Subject-Object relationship defines developmental growth. Aspects of experience, such as thoughts, feelings, and behaviours, are considered as 'Object' when one is capable of taking a third-person perspective on one's first-person experience. This transition to an objective perspective is a marker of increasing complexity of mind. The individual can now observe and reflect about that to which they were once Subject.

Subject. ("I am")

This is our blind area. Things that are in Subject cannot be seen and are by definition experienced as unquestioned, simply a part of the self. Because they can't be seen, they are taken for granted, taken for true—or not even taken at all. You generally can't name things that are Subject - that would require the ability to stand back and take a look at them. You don't have something that's Subject; something that's Subject has you. They include personality traits; creative adaptations, social conditioning and the way its influenced your core beliefs; big assumptions about who you are and the way the world works; your behaviours and emotions.

Object. ("I have")

While things that are in Subject have you, you have things that are now in Object. The more of your life experience you have as Object, the more complex your worldview because you can see and act upon more things. It may also reduce the risk of you becoming snagged by unfinished business or acting out of old patterns. The very fact that these things are now visible and known to you means that you have choice about how you act and feel. You can detach, reflect on and take greater control over your ways of being in the world.

Kegan's stage descriptors

The Self-Sovereign Mind (many adolescents and a small number of adults)

The emphasis at this stage is on one's own needs, interests and agendas. These are primary, and can sometimes be experienced by others (parents for instance) as the only focus.

Relationships are often transactional and individuals at this stage view people as a means to get their own needs met, as opposed to a shared internal experience (how we feel about each other). They care about how others perceive them, but only because those perceptions may have concrete consequences for them. For example, friends do not lie to each other, it is because of a fear of the consequences or retaliation, not because they value honesty and transparency in a relationship.

Moreover, individuals follow along with rules, philosophies, movements or ideologies because of external rewards or punishments, not because they truly believe in them.

The developmental movement from this more egocentric level into the socialised mind has been described by Kegan as a 'triumph of development'. The adults alongside, especially parents, breathe a big sigh of relief. They've joined the adult world and are equipped to get along in it. There's still lots of learning and challenges ahead around work, loving relationships, intimacy and connection but sufficient preparation has happened and they're ready enough for all that.

The Socialised Mind (older adolescents and the majority of adults)

At this stage, the most important things are the ideas, norms, morals and beliefs of the people and systems around us - family, society, ideology and culture – external sources. We begin to experience ourselves as a function of how others experience us so we internalise the feelings and emotions of others and are guided by those people or institutions that are most important to us. We are shaped by the expectations of those around us. What we think and say is strongly influenced by what we think others want to hear. There is a pull to belong and fit in. We look for external validation to derive our sense of self. Relationships occupy the central place and how they are going, defines our well-being.

Unlike people at the earlier self-sovereign stage, we no longer view other people as a means to an end. We can internalise others' perspectives and actually care about others' opinions of us—not just with regards to the consequences of those opinions. For example: I care that you're angry with me because I care about you and our relationship, not just because if you're angry then you won't invite me to your party.

We are able to think abstractly, be self-reflective about our actions and the actions of others, and are devoted to something that's greater than our own needs.

However, at this stage our awareness of how our goals and behaviours are still predetermined by others and by our culture may be fairly limited. We don't yet recognise the extent to which we are defined from the outside in. Our life appears to be self-authored, but that's because we do not yet see how we are continuing to follow the dictates of family and cultural conditioning as voiced by parents, bosses, teachers, friends and spouses. We are yet to examine this because it's largely invisible to us.

Kegan points out that the very notion of "self-esteem" is inappropriate at this stage because self-esteem implies an internal source for feeling good about oneself. Those at this stage don't have an independently-constructed self to feel good about; their esteem is entirely reliant on others because they are, in many ways, made up of those around them.

In Garvey Berger's view: "The socialised mind was probably perfect for much of history – as we had relatively clear boundaries, and clear roles to play. Humans lived in smaller, more homogenous societies, and there were clear rules and clear leaders."

A major limitation of this stage now is that, many of those clear directions and codes have disappeared. The old stories don't hold anymore, the rule books are being re-written, and this has left many people disoriented and bewildered. The Outside is failing to provide the answers to the Inside.

The Self-Authored Mind (some adults)

At this stage, we have achieved all that those at the previous stage have, but have now created a self that exists even outside of its relationship to others. The opinions and desires of others which we internalized and which had great control over us when we were making meaning at the socialised stage are now Object to us. We are now able to examine those various rule-systems and opinions and are able to mediate between them. We now have an internal set of rules and regulations—a self-governing system—which we use to make our decisions or mediate conflicts. We can feel empathy for others, and take the wishes and opinions of others into consideration when making decisions. At this stage, we don't feel as torn apart by the conflicts of those around us because we have our own system with which to make decisions.

At this stage we "own" our work, are self-guided, self-motivated, self evaluative, have our own ideology (which can be a positive and negative), and our own internal compass to guide ourselves. We have freed ourselves up from some of the earlier, restrictive shoulds and oughts that we internalised when younger. We understand our own values and we can take stands.

The Self-Transforming Mind (very few adults)

Adults at this stage have achieved all that those at the earlier stages have, but have learned the limits of their own inner belief system—and the limits of having an inner system in general. Instead of viewing others as people with separate and different inner systems, at this stage we see across inner systems to look at the similarities that are hidden inside what used to look like differences. We are less likely to see the world in terms of polarities and are more likely to believe that what we often think of as black and white are just various shades of grey whose differences are made more visible by the lighter or darker colours around them.

So, at this stage, we have our own ideology, but can more easily step back from it and see it as limited and at best, partial. We can hold complexity, opposites, contradictions and ambiguity. Either-or thinking is replaced by both-and.

Ego maturity and action logics definitions

As you read through the following definitions you may see yourself, and others you know well, in several categories. This shouldn't be surprising given that the previous developmental stages we've progressed through continue to be nested within us. Whilst we predominantly 'live' at our 'middle' stage or level (centre of gravity), we regress at times of insecurity, stress and illness to a previous stage; just as we glimpse ourselves operating at the next stage during optimal conditions, maximum support and periods of transition.

These definitions should be considered as best approximations rather than perfectly accurate. However, it should also be recognised that they are the result of many years of research by a number of thought-leaders in the field of adult development and as you get to grips with them, I believe you will find some very enlightening and thought-provoking messages.

And if you find the definitions describing the conventional and early postconventional stages more familiar, don't be surprised. The research shows that the vast majority of adults 'live here'. The consequence of that is the quality of definitions relating to the late postconventional stages – Construct-aware/Alchemist and beyond - may seem less developed due in large part to the relatively small number of people identified there.

The meaning of action logics

Action logics refers to the meaning-making capacities that shape how we meet, engage, understand, and respond to the world and our experiences, Hayton (2018).

They...

1. Represent the way we organise reality, or more accurately our understanding of reality.

2. Describe the developmental stage of meaning-making that informs and drives our reasoning and behaviour.

3. Include our sense of identity, what we see as the purpose of life, what needs we act upon, what ends we are moving toward, our emotions and experience of being in the world, and how we think about ourselves and the world.

It's important to understand that each action logic emerges from a synthesis of doing, being (experiencing and feeling), and thinking despite the term logic, which may suggest an emphasis on cognition (thinking).

Cook-Greuter's and Torbert/Rooke's definitions

Having begun with some of Kegan's key concepts and stage definitions, I now focus on the terminology from the Cook-Greuter ego maturity framework (self-centric, group-centric, skill-centric etc); the Torbert & Rooke action logics framework (Diplomat, Expert, Achiever etc), and refer to the equivalent colour code from Spiral Dynamics (Graves, Beck & Cowan). I also include the nearest equivalent stage definitions from Kegan to create a more comprehensive map. To see a visual representation of all of these frameworks at-a-glance, see the table at the end of this article entitled 'Developmental frameworks – a map of the territory'.

Self-Centric/Opportunist/Red

Note, that in the Kegan framework this would be the self-sovereign stage of consciousness.

The self-centric mind seeks to outsmart its opponents. Egocentric, the focus at this stage is on looking after one's own needs, security and self-protection. It's me who matters. Will try to win by any means possible. What you can get away with is 'right'. The world and other people are opportunities to be exploited. Their tendency is to treat people in a transactional way and seek control or even dominance. They project onto others the same perception of life that they themselves hold and make the assumption that others are also looking to manipulate, control and exploit. They perceive those who take a more positive, optimistic, liberal worldview to be naïve or even a potential 'mark'. A 'regular' person would describe someone at this stage as a 'chancer' or a 'cowboy'. If you can get away with it, do it. 'Might is right', business is war, 'grab' your opportunities, land the first punch, are all watchwords of people at this stage. They prefer action and concrete tasks to ideas and theoretical discussions, which they often dismiss as wishy-washy.

Can have a fragile sense of self, which explains the need to be self-protective, and feel that they are the odd one out – me against the rest of the world. This can lead to a hyper-vigilance and regular loss of self-control. When things go wrong the central tendency is to blame and scape-goat others. Feedback can be experienced as attack, resulting in angry feelings. If given a leadership role (which is increasingly rare in multi-nationals and global corporates), is likely to adopt a more dictatorial, coercive style. Very demanding of others, and demanding of loyalty. Subordinates are likely to feel oppressed, ridiculed or bullied, unless they're a favourite. Humour can be hostile and used to put others down. Trust and mistrust are common themes. Trouble often follows self-centric/opportunists and leaders at this action logic are usually visible and under pressure to change behaviours – some will be in 'last chance saloon'. Change, or you go. External coaches are sometimes brought in to give it one more attempt but will usually come to the conclusion that this is a low coachability scenario.

On the other hand, they can be invaluable in dangerous situations where they will have a nose for trouble – and also in emergencies. Can sometimes be seen as likeable but somewhat immature rogues. In the work context, they can be tolerated because they're 'savvy' at spotting sales opportunities and if teamed up with similar people who enjoy sailing close to the wind may be commercially successful – and even surpass their colleagues. The collateral damage, however, usually catches up with them.

If we return to the Russian dolls metaphor used earlier, we should remember that somewhere in our nested experience we all have an 'inner opportunist'. And at times that can be useful. If we find ourselves in an unsafe environment, or the target of a scam where we could become a victim, it's best that we quickly realise it and find ways to protect ourselves.

Group-centric/Diplomat/Amber

Note, that in the Kegan framework this would be the socialised stage of consciousness.

Sometimes this stage is also known as Conformist. It's about trying to get it right for others, often holding back or holding in ones' own thoughts, feelings and needs. Group-centric/diplomats seek approval to minimise inner and outer conflict. They want to belong to the group and demonstrate socially accepted behaviour; so rarely rock the boat. Instead, they try to be pleasant and agreeable preferring not to stand out as different, even when having a different view. May therefore hold back their own contributions. Diplomats define themselves not from the inside-out, but from the outside-in, thereby needing external validation for their self-worth. I am my relationships is the primary self-definition and this means that those relationships must be protected. With a tendency to generalise, gloss-over disagreements and try to placate, diplomats can be smothering. In organisational life diplomats are often referred to assertiveness training courses and may be encouraged to challenge more and put themselves more at the centre of their lives. This runs entirely contrary to their core assumptions which explains why so often these programmes don't work so well with people at this action logic. In management roles, they are likely to find the expectation of holding courageous, honest conversations with colleagues highly threatening and will seek to avoid them if at all possible.

Diplomats often struggle with ambiguity, the grey of life, preferring and in some cases needing a high level of clarity about what is expected and what the rules and norms are. When that clarity isn't forthcoming it can heighten anxiety.

On the other hand, diplomats are good as supportive glue; helping bring people together, and keeping the mood positive. They pay attention to the needs of others and keep an eye out for people who may be struggling.

Given that approval is such a key psychological theme, diplomats can hear feedback as disapproval and feel hurt by it. Can be uncomfortable and reluctant to give feedback unless it's positive and don't like being asked to 'evaluate' another person which they can interpret as judging.

Some teams, and some families, are held together by managers, team members, parents and siblings whose centre of gravity is at diplomat. They can be invaluable when situations need a soothing, re-assuring presence.

Skill-centric/Expert/Amber

Note, that in the Kegan framework this would also be the socialised stage of consciousness.

It's about my knowledge, expertise, competence and capacity to fix and problem-solve. Studies show that there are many people at this stage in management and leadership roles. Skill-centric, expert capacity is essential for running the routine affairs of every society and business. It's especially important in today's highly technological and digital world. Experts are typically immersed in their craft logic – the specific procedures, knowledge and expertise of their area. Their identity is meshed with their knowledge and skills. Motivated to stand out as competent which provides a sense of control, they seek rational efficiency. Unsurprisingly, many accountants, engineers, technocrats and teachers operate from this action logic. Experts value correctness based on authority, (technical knowledge, famous scholars etc) and strive towards the right answer or best way of thinking and acting. Can be critical and competitive with others. The yes, but syndrome and a tendency for one-upmanship is very common coming out of strong belief systems and opinions. Can be dogmatic and not easily deflected from what they believe to be right. In organisations, experts often associate management with admin, will seek to avoid management roles and won't always appreciate the value or significance of leadership.

Experts often have lots of unexamined 'shoulds' and oughts'. Their decisions are made on incontrovertible facts, and can be stuck in perfectionism. Cognitive intelligence (being bright) trumps emotional intelligence which is often not rated highly. The human dimension can be missed, relationships may not be prioritised, detail may obscure the bigger picture. Experts are not naturals for personal growth and development unless they get interested in the art and science of it (the craft expertise).

Often take great pride in their work and finding incremental improvements to processes. Good as an individual contributor and problem-solver when the issue is technical. At the extreme, can act like a solution looking for a problem. They typically believe there's a predictable solution to all problems. Others who 'know less' on the subject can be dismissed; their thoughts and feelings can seem like a distraction or nuisance. Can struggle to hear feedback and get defensive unless it's coming from an even more expert, expert.

Self-determining/Achiever/Orange

Note, that in the Kegan framework this would be the self-authored stage of consciousness.

Self-determining/achievers have a strong singularity of purpose, focus and drive. They like to be in charge, initiate, get things done and move on to the next thing. Planning, managing people, tasks and information, and seeking to stay in control of it all; that's the nature of their world. When that sense of control starts to slip, they can be susceptible to stress, anxiety and panic.

Achievers are effective at meeting goals through other people and teams; juggling managerial duties with stakeholder demands. Well suited to managerial roles; action and goal oriented, achievers enjoy agency and the greater control and autonomy of leadership. More able to listen to others and see things from the others perspective, they often enjoy coaching, story-telling and teaching.

Achievers often drive themselves hard, have a pace-setting leadership style and have a high fear of failure. Can be self-critical, prone to excessive guilt when standards, including their own, are not met and are often their own worst critics.

Being over-extended and maintaining balance are common issues, and in more extreme scenarios, the feeling of being overwhelmed is present together with the danger of burnout. Internally, they feel like they've lost the 'off button', and find it difficult to slow down and live in the present moment. The impact of their achiever workstyle on those closest to them can become problematic because they're always working or distracted, and have very little left for their primary relationships. The classic picture of always on a device and the fear of missing out can mean that they are there, but not really there.

Increasingly open to development, they go looking for behavioural feedback to continuously improve, accomplish more, achieve their goals and feel a greater sense of control. They may still resist anything that suggests there's more to life than achievement though this can change if they begin to craft a new life purpose or reframe their raison d'etre as fulfilment and enjoyment.

The self-determining/achiever action logic is the last stage of conventional adult development and is the target stage for Western culture. Together, with experts, they comprise just under 70% of managers and leaders in organisational life. Those who are beginning to transition from here are entering what is known as the postconventional tier.

Self-questioning/Individualist/Green

Note, that in the Kegan framework this would be the self-authored stage of consciousness.

This is seen by some as a transitional action logic and by others as the first postconventional action logic. It often emerges out of some kind of awakening experience. This can be a life experience, perhaps a crisis, or a consciousness-raising developmental process such as a personal growth retreat, working with a psychologically skilled coach or going into therapy. It may also be accelerated by greater exposure to people with postconventional worldviews.

Often more reflective, questioning and contemplative, individualists are more likely to be aware of their interior world and interested in the inner experience of others. At this stage, relational skills tend to be stronger along with heightened emotional awareness and the capacity to empathise. There can also be a growing appreciation of their shadow, and how it impacts. Individualists are more likely to be searching and open to development as an end in itself rather than a means to an end. There is often an increased understanding of complexity and unintended, problematic consequences of actions.

At this stage, people are less interested in facts, knowledge and expertise. They are beginning to develop a systems perspective and are less linear in their thinking. They are also more self-questioning around assumptions, values, purpose and beliefs. There is greater capacity to adjust own presence and behaviours to the context. Individualists often ignore rules that they regard as irrelevant or creating an obstacle; a behaviour pattern that can irritate colleagues who are playing by the rules. Can come up with new thinking and create unique structures to resolve the gap between declared strategy and real-world performance. This capacity to think creatively and outside the box can mean that they're treated as a special case.

And their different way of seeing the way forward, combined with their willingness to take risks, can mean that they use their leadership role to create new, interesting roles for others and cultivate company sub-cultures where some of the normal constraints are lifted – allowing people and things to move faster.

At times Individualists can seem like they've lost their compass and may even have lost their desire. Despite continuing to achieve and reach goals, their sense of identity is no longer meshed with doing and achievement. This can be disconcerting to achiever colleagues. On the other hand, it can be fun to have this person around - their individuality and distance from the common agenda can look attractive on some days and frustrating or threatening on others. Are they really committed?

Sometimes they unhook from their organisational roles to follow a different career path. It's not unusual to find them moving into start-ups and consulting roles. Some make significant life changes to follow their passion and purpose. And for others, their passion is to stay in the organisation and change it – to use their leadership role and enhanced personal capacity to transform the place they know.

Self-actualising/Strategist /Teal

Note, that in the Kegan framework this would be the self-transforming stage of consciousness.

The strategist can be identified by their vision, quality of thinking and perspective, their emotional maturity and their wisdom. Their wisdom shows up in many ways, not least their deeper appreciation for multiple-realities and multiple perspectives. They are increasingly aware of paradox and contradiction, both in themselves and in the world.

Strategists are increasingly guided by principles which inform their actions, such as seeking mutuality of power with colleagues. They no longer have an issue with sharing power as they recognise whilst they may be in charge; they will never be in control as this is an illusion.

Whilst they have let go of the need for autonomy associated with earlier stages they appreciate other's need for it. Their preference is for collaborative working and tend to be welcoming of difference.

Whereas in earlier stages individuals often have a tendency to see the world from an 'I' perspective, and later from a 'we' perspective, the strategist goes beyond their immediate 'we' of family, team and close friends, to the much larger 'us' of organisation or beyond. Their perspective and their primary concerns have moved beyond an egocentric and group-centric perspective to take into consideration a larger worldview.

A defining characteristic of strategists is that they are capable of generating organisational and personal transformations. They are therefore deemed to be effective as transformational leaders. But, as with alchemists at the next stage, these postconventional leaders don't transform organisations (or whole societies in the case of some Alchemists) just for the sake of it. Such leaders possess a purposefully transformational worldview (Akrivou & Bradbury-Huang 2011).

This evolving sense of purpose both motivates themselves and also inspires others —so it's simultaneously personally fulfilling and empowering. These individuals who tend to be highly curious and open to new experiences are more likely to search for and live out their purpose in life, Kashdan & McKnight (2009).

They seek feedback from others as vital for growth and making sense of the world.

When leaders are inspired by a deeply meaningful (Reker & Wong 2012) purpose that, in turn, can inspire employees, team members, or other followers, organisations benefit from the unifying sense of direction that purpose can provide. In this way, an individual's purpose may even become an organisation's mission (Bronk & McLean 2016).

Construct-aware/Alchemist. Turquoise

We should recognise that most people have never spent time with anyone at this stage of adult maturity. Even those who work regularly with leaders, as fellow-leaders, or coaches and consultants to them, may never have met one.

In the Torbert &Rooke studies they report that 'Alchemists constitute 1% of our sample, which indicates how rare it is to find them in business or anywhere else. Our studies of the few leaders we have identified as alchemists suggest that what sets them apart from strategists is their ability to renew or even reinvent themselves and their organisations in historically significant ways. Whereas the strategist will move from one engagement to another, the alchemist has an extraordinary capacity to deal simultaneously with many situations at multiple levels'.

It may be more likely to find people operating at this stage of adult development outside of organisational life as their purpose can be more about personal and spiritual transformation and supporting others in their life quests.

Alchemists often have bigger missions altogether and have a commitment to changing the society and institutions in which they participate or the genre they work in. Historically, some well-known social catalysts and visionaries may have been in this category. People such as Martin Luther King, Mahatma Gandhi, Nelson Mandela and Joan of Arc are often referred to in this light although, self-evidently, this may not be the case as they were not the subject of sophisticated profiling assessments. All these people attracted dedicated supporters, and posthumous accolades as well as outright adversaries during their own time. They threatened and disturbed the status quo evoking powerful and often polarised feelings in those around them. Some inspired devotional love and to this day stand as inspirational figures. Their lives were often a triumph of courage amidst great pain and suffering.

Stage transition issues

The most common transitions observable in organisational life are between expert and achiever (a high number of managers profiled using stage assessment instruments are in transition between expert and achiever); and achiever to individualist. In Kegan's language, this is the journey towards self-authoring and consolidating at this stage.

More attention is now being placed on the individualist to strategist stage transition as it's considered vital that we accelerate the pace at which this happens in order to have more leaders at this later stage. (More on this in a later chapter).

Expert to Achiever transition

For many people in organisational life, the stretch out from the expert centre of gravity to achiever is not deeply unsettling; indeed, it can be welcomed as a sign of career progression providing higher financial reward, more responsibility, greater autonomy and capacity to influence. New roles often offer greater opportunity to engage in strategic thinking and it can be experienced as genuinely arriving – the chance to really show people what you can do.

However, for others, their attachment to knowing, problem-solving and fixing things can be a barrier to making a full transition. Their self-definition is around rational thought and argument, allied with technical capability, and this is what provides their deeper sense of significance and value. The fear of having to let that go and discover meaning through a different, less clear route, should not be under-estimated. This can lead to some people staying 'on-the-tools', rejecting opportunities to progress into management and leadership roles.

Typically, there's also a developmental challenge around seeing the inner game, as Tim Gallwey (2000) describes it, as well as the outer game. Outer game is usually what's in Object for experts; their inner game, and the inner experience of others, can still be in Subject. Self-development that awakens people to reflection and the appreciation that many of life's problems and challenges won't be solved by outer game, technical solutions, only by adaptive change, can have a transformative impact on their transition.

But it's not just experts who may have a developmental journey to make around 'inner knowing' and the capacity to empathetically tune into others. This can also be an issue at achiever and individualist stages. The capacity to really listen to self and others takes many people a long time to develop. At the postconventional stages, it's more likely that people will have acquired a more sophisticated understanding of the inner as well as outer games of life. This may have happened through wider life experiences and access to the kinds of developmental experiences that accelerate vertical development, such as deep-dive programmes, developmental coaching and late stage mentors.

Another very different reason why experts don't always make this transition is that they can build up a great deal of credibility in their organisations for their expertise, as well as high financial reward. Some have also learned to make full use of this to consolidate their positions and appear untouchable. In this case, there may be little incentive to grow and develop; other than in horizontal ways.

Achiever to Individualist transition

Consolidation at the achiever stage can take several years and the research findings indicate that most people don't make the transition to individualist and beyond. They may show glimpses of an emerging worldview and display some of the behaviours and perspectives associated with that. But they stay at the late achiever action logic. That's their plateau.

Whereas the expert is attached to their knowledge and know-how, the challenge for the achiever is to lessen their attachment to power, control and success. It's no accident that most airport bookshops are full of books on 'winning'. Achievers are seen fair game for the latest work/life success formulas.

Those who do make this transition, and it's only a small minority of leaders, often experience it as more unsettling than previous transitions. They tend to have more questions, the kind with no easy answers. They are often about purpose, (am I really doing what I should be?), self-worth, meaning of life, and way of life.

This transition can also feel more risky, lonely and more psychologically complex. You are likely to be re-thinking things, and maybe re-organizing your life. Relationship dynamics can go through significant changes.

Following your own path can mean disappointing others – important others who you feel loyalty towards and indebted to. You may also feel more at odds with rules and codes that were previously invisible or less important to you. Conventional life looks different and you may feel inclined to challenge more of it. This is the fuller meaning behind Kegan's notion of the self-authored mind.

If you are in this transition you are likely to find several of these inner driving forces for vertical development pertinent to you.

- A desire to understand yourself better and discover your life vision/purpose.

- Wanting to create a life consistent with your highest aspirations and what you care most about.

- Wanting to make a different kind of contribution: for example, to build the confidence and capacity of those around you. In the work environment, this will include your teams and wider organisation. It may also include your family, friends and community.

- Regularly experiencing the limits of your current way of thinking, reacting and trying to solve things.

- Repetitive patterns or historic shadow issues negatively impacting in the present.

- The sense of having outgrown a level and a need to breakthrough.

- Being in pain (existential).

You will probably notice that there are two kinds of qualitatively different driving forces here: the earlier ones are around fulfilment of potential, self-improvement and living your purpose. These are positive, forward-looking, bold statements of personal intent. They reflect a desire and energy to stretch yourself – to push your frontier and be all you can be. These are often referred to as our leading edge - who you want to become and where you want to go.

Other kinds of driving forces, those later ones in the list, emerge out of tensions, dissonance or pain – a sense of things not being as you would want them to be. Or more accurately, you not being how you want to be. It can arise from a crisis, a challenge or a set of problems that you don't seem to be able to resolve from your current worldview. Developmental theorists point out that movement from one adult development stage to the next is usually driven by limitations in the current stage. When you are confronted with increased complexity and challenge that can't be met with what you know and can do at your current level, you are pulled to take the next step (McGuire & Rhodes, 2009).

Some of these can be seen as our trailing edge – the heavy rucksack as the poet Robert Bly described that we spend our life carrying – and hoping in time to empty.

Neither is intrinsically better nor worse than the other, although the leading edge will tend to feel better. Our hopes, aspirations and desires to be our best self are worthy and important. But we also have our struggles and it's OK to be troubled. It's both of these that makes us who we are.

Relationship issues arising from different worldviews

What we see

One of the most compelling arguments for a developmental perspective is that it helps people make more sense of why colleagues they work with sometimes view the world so very differently to themselves. What others see, and the meaning they make of it, can be so different that you sometimes find yourself saying – 'why didn't they see it'? or 'how on earth did they get to that?', or 'why on earth did they react (over-react) like that?

And it's not just about what people see and don't see. It's also about what really matters most to them, and consequently, what they give most attention to - which can be quite different to what's most important to you.

Vertical development theory can help us understand why such different interpretations of the same so-called 'realities' take place so often. People see what they see through their lens on life, their worldview, and their meaning-making follows from that. But it's not just what we see, it's also what we can't see. These are the elements in any given situation that are still in Subject, to use Kegan's language. And this has huge implications for relationships, in the workplace relationships and wider life.

Sometimes people don't 'get it', because they simply can't. And sometimes they don't 'get you', for the very same reason. We might ascribe intention to their failure to see things the way we do, but that's often not the real reason. They are not actively resisting you, although that does happen sometimes. It's more a question of multiple perspectives arising from what people can presently take a viewpoint on.

So, one of your ever-present challenges, as a manager, leader or coach, is to get a better sense of what people can see and take a perspective on; get a better sense of what they can't yet see; calibrate your communication accordingly; and encourage a growth mindset where they get more curious and want to learn and grow. Then developmental shifts and breakthroughs are within reach. You're expanding the possible.

Tension points arising from different worldviews and frames of reference

Note that these are approximations rather than truths – they do not define people. Rather, they shed some light on what may still be invisible to us. That is, the ways in which someone's developmental stage manifests in their behavioural repertoire, what they regard as most important and what is of less interest to them. These represent significant differences in the way people are, and have important implications for working together, and wider life relationships.

- The self-centric/opportunist worldview prioritises number one. The consequence can be a dilution of trust by seeming to be 'on the make' or on the look-out to take advantage. People tend to be wary of opportunists and keep their guard up.

- The group-centric/diplomat's worldview is located in the desire to belong and please. This can lead to compliant behaviour and fence-sitting, avoiding the difficult conversations for fear of upsetting people. This can be experienced by others as inauthentic. People with this frame of reference often want a level of clarity about what's expected of them that can frustrate their managers and colleagues. They can be uncomfortable with ambiguity – the grey, as it's often referred to in organisations. Achievers and postconventional managers can lose patience with their need for direction and answers. Their own trajectory has taken them towards a greater sense of independence and autonomy and they may have forgotten that they also wanted more certainty themselves in the past.

- Skill-centric/experts can be perceived as overly perfectionist, stuck in detail and not sufficiently interested in the bigger picture; perhaps refusing, or seeking to avoid, management roles and responsibilities. This "I" perspective on the world can be a friction point with achievers where pace, good-enough and the team ethos ("we") are considered as more important. Experts are not the most reflective of people, can also be seen as not listening well enough, nor sufficiently interested in others experience. Combine this with a tendency to think they know best and you have a recipe for tensions.

- The self-determining/achiever's tendency to over-commit, find it difficult to switch off and be in the present moment without doing, doing, doing, can have a powerful impact on their core relationships. They can give the impression that anything other than pace, action and results doesn't register as valuable in their eyes. In turn, this can limit the range of conversations that become possible.

- Whilst people may value the out-of-the-box, innovative thinking that individualists are capable of, sometimes their ideas can be seen as too weird. There can also be a perception that individualists are ultimately not team players, preferring to do their own thing. Their need for autonomy can also leave an impression that they regard themselves and wish to be treated as special cases.

- Experts and achievers can experience individualists and strategists as aloof or out of touch with the practical realities of life (on another wavelength, or another planet, as they see it).

- Reactions to feedback have also been found to vary according to developmental stage. Opportunists will often experience feedback as attack; diplomats can feel a sense for personal disapproval; and experts can experience feedback as criticism unless the feedback-giver is a 'true expert' in their eyes.

Drawing on previous stage perspectives

As outlined in chapter 1, 'Adult development theory', we operate most of the time from our current centre of gravity, our highest and most complex meaning-making system, glimpsing the next stage in optimal circumstances, and regressing to at least one back in times of stress and illness, However, it's important to remember the metaphor of the Russian dolls, where each previous stage remains nested within us. The reason why this is so important is that this is a dynamic theory and human beings are not static beings. We are multi-faceted with a multitude of mind-sets.

Even during the course of this morning, as I've combined my writing of this chapter with several business and family involvements, I've noticed myself reacting, or nearly reacting, from several worldviews. At one point, I was certainly accessing my best self, but I was also triggered and re-stimulated by issues that took me back to earlier ways of reacting and seeing the world.

In other words, we all have our inner opportunist, diplomat, expert, and so on. If you find yourself there, don't be surprised. What matters, if you've been triggered, is to develop the capacity to know when it's happening and make it a short visit. This capacity for self-awareness, and being able to observe yourself in action, is critical to more mature behaviour.

And let's also remember that re-visiting our earlier stages is not just a matter of regression. In certain circumstances, the choiceful use of our opportunist, where there's danger and insecurity; the intentional use of our diplomat presence to calm troubled waters; the expertise and knowledge so vital to all areas of life; and the accomplishment of objectives that will always be a fundamental part of our lives.

Developmental frameworks – a map of the territory

A summary of several prominent adult development frameworks

Kegan	Cook-Greuter	Wilbur	Graves, Beck and Cowan	Torbert and Rooke	Maslow	Worldview
	Unitive	Ironist	Indigo	Ironist (<1%)		
Self-transforming (<5%)	Construct aware	Magician	Turquoise	Alchemist (2%)	Self transcendence	Post-conventional
	Self-actualising	Strategist	Teal	Strategist (4%)	Self-actualisation	Post-conventional
Self-authored (35%)	Self-questioning	Individualist	Green	Individualist (10%)		Post-conventional
	Self determining	Achiever	Orange	Achiever (30%)		Conventional
Socialised (58%)	Skill-centric	Expert	Amber	Expert (38%)	Self-esteem	Conventional
	Group-centric	Diplomat		Diplomat (12%)	Belonging	Conventional
Self-sovereign (7%)	Self-centric	Opportunistic impulsive	Red	Opportunist (5%)	Safety Physiological	Pre-conventional
Form of mind	Ego development	Integral	Spiral dynamics	Action logics	Needs	

3.
Horizontal learning and vertical development

- Introduction
- Horizontal learning
- Vertical development
- A summary of vertical development propositions
- Vertical development applied to organisational leadership

Introduction

When we approach the subject of human, evolutionary development, we need to distinguish between horizontal and vertical development. Horizontal learning happens through schooling, higher education, training, structured programmes and self-directed learning. It also occurs through living our lives, if we reflect and assimilate the learning from our own experiences.

Susanne Cook-Greuter, a thought-leader in the adult development field, shows the difference between horizontal and vertical development in this graphic. Most growth is of a horizontal kind with expansion occurring through new information, skills and processes. When people attend professional training courses, seminars and developmental workshops they invariably say that they are hoping to get more tools, techniques and models. Despite having already got a huge stock of these in many cases, they still travel in the hope and expectation that there will be another one somewhere that somehow surpasses all the others or brings the whole picture together. That new nugget of gold.

The big question that Cook-Greuter and others have posed, is whether this fundamentally changes the person's mental framework and worldview. Horizontal learning is essential, but is additive, fitting into a person's current paradigm. In essence, it involves learning more of the same thing to produce increased breadth, refinement and differentiation of existing knowledge and skill. It doesn't transform their action logic or level of consciousness. That happens through a different process known as vertical development which at this point in human evolution, is far less understood and practiced - unless you've been exposed to the modern psychological disciplines or much older wisdom traditions.

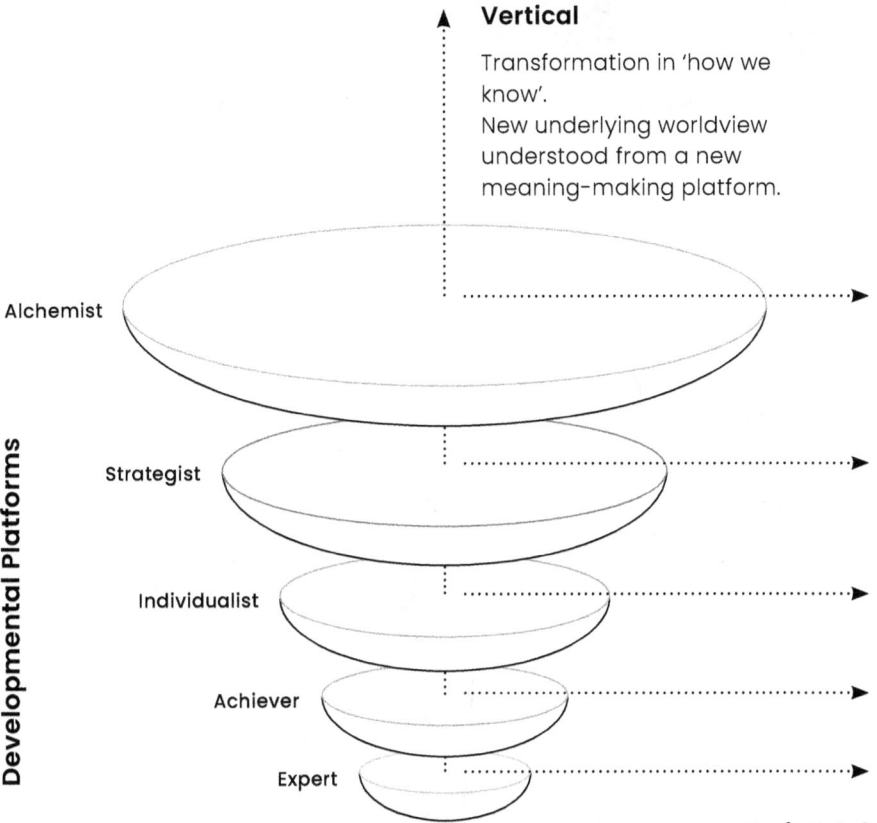

Vertical

Transformation in 'how we know'.
New underlying worldview understood from a new meaning-making platform.

Developmental Platforms

Alchemist

Strategist

Individualist

Achiever

Expert

Horizontal

Expansion in 'what we know' (new skills, new information, new knowledge) but understood from the same meaning-making platform.

Horizontal learning

Recent interest in horizontal and vertical development has brought to people's attention that most leadership development processes, and learning in general, has been based on the premise that if we equip people with knowledge, new skills, abilities and behaviours, then those will later translate into improved competency and performance. This paradigm is a technical one where problems can be broken down, analysed and fixed so long as we have acquired the necessary technical knowledge to deal with them.

An analogy frequently used to describe horizontal development is the act of pouring water into a glass. As more knowledge, skills and competencies are acquired, the glass fills up. When deficits are identified, the answer is to find new or better ones to put into the glass. People who search for new tools, techniques and models are effectively on the same mission - to fill their glass. From this perspective, excellence in management and leadership, or for that matter, any form of practice, is achieved by filling the glass with the best possible content available.

How vertical compliments horizontal

Horizontal development =

adding more knowledge, skills and competencies. (Filling the glass with more content)

Vertical approaches =

grows the internal capacities to operate in more complex, systemic, strategic and interdependent ways.

Expands an individual's ability to handle complexity and 'sense make' in ambiguous and uncertain situations. (Increases the glass size or leader's worldview)

Given that most education systems, professional and leadership development programmes are based on the horizontal paradigm, it's hardly surprising that many people only understand learning and development from this point of view. And it would be absurd to dismiss the importance of knowledge acquisition and proper training to perform proficiently. Business managers need to understand profit and loss accounts, company procedures and good HR practice. Leaders need to understand how to turn around the financial performance of their organisations and enable them to flourish. Core skills, informational content and technical expertise are all required in any professional discipline. Without it people would flounder or worse still, make disastrous mistakes. So, it goes without saying that horizontal learning is necessary and is important at each and every stage of adult development. It expands the breadth of one's information, knowledge, and skills.

However, the image of the two glasses makes the powerful point; that whilst traditional, horizontal learning fills the glass, vertical growth and development increases the size of the glass. We literally become more spacious, bigger people.

Vertical development

Who looks outside, dreams,
Who looks inside, awakens – Jung

Vertical development is the process of learning to see the world through new eyes and changing the interpretations and meanings we ascribe to life experience. It largely requires an inside-out approach to learning, quite different in nature to the outside-in horizontal method. Vertical development is based on reflection, awareness-raising and personal insight, and requires a deeper self-examination. In turn, this can lead to changes in perspective and an increased capacity to see, understand, empathise, and be in stronger contact with ourselves, others and the world.

It's important to recognise that horizontal and vertical development paths are not an either-or. On the contrary, they work together. Skill and knowledge from horizontal development often require reflective practice and feedback which can then lead to increased awareness. Combining this with a willingness to be changed by awareness and experience, critical to vertical development, can transform how we come to know ourselves and influence our world.

When individuals evolve to a later stage of adult development it is the result of both horizontal learning and vertical development – the acquisition of knowledge, skills and behaviours together with psychological, emotional and spiritual development. This is a virtuous circle in that inner change alters outer behaviours. For example, as a person matures, deals with more of their shadow and unfinished situations, we generally see less defensiveness and volatility, the need to control and be right, or to offer uninvited opinions and advice.

Letting go

In contrast to horizontal learning, vertical development is as much about unlearning as learning. Indeed, one of its key features, and an important reason why it's so difficult, is that it so often involves letting go of something. And in turn that produces a felt sense that we're at risk – we're going to lose someone or something.

Loss, and the fear of it, combined with the vulnerability that's associated with it, is part of the vertical development terrain. It can be the letting go of certainty, and a re-assessment of strongly held beliefs and assumptions. Or the loss of previous ways of seeing the world. But it's not so much that these were wrong; rather, we come to see that they were incomplete.

It can be letting go of the identity we've formed around something we've created. Or the letting go of the story we re-tell about ourselves which we've come to realise is no longer accurate, or even true. It can be letting go of our need to look good, to control or be right.

Perhaps the most powerful and difficult thing many of us need to let go is our habit of living with excessive fear, self-doubt and an over-sized inner critic. And to replace that with a kinder, more gentle and compassionate relationship with ourselves.

None of this is easy but by letting go, our perspective evolves and we change. And we may discover that we can travel lighter into our futures.

The process of vertical development involves inner change, psychological breakthroughs and emotional contact, and is not always visible to the untrained eye. Sometimes it's only months or years later that people notice and say – there's something different about you now.

Cognitive understanding of vertical development can be a useful starting point and may create a shift of consciousness. However, on its own, it's unlikely to be enough. The journey of vertical development is primarily an experiential one. So, just as reading about emotional intelligence doesn't necessarily lead to an improvement in EQ, reading about developmental theory doesn't transition a person to the next stage nor fundamentally change their centre of gravity.

To grow a more conscious mind often begins with freeing the mind. Many of us know that we are still captured by a combination of the external circumstances of our lives and historical unfinished experiences that continue to be re-stimulated in present time.

If we are still locked into the technical worldview where every problem and dilemma can be broken down, analysed and fixed in the same way as engineering issues can be resolved, then we may run the risk of wasting a great of our energy and time going around and around the same spirals. Many of life's more complex and challenging problems are of a different nature and require a very different approach to them – adaptive change. A change in ourselves. That's not to say there aren't times when we do need to alter some of those material circumstances of our life to become freed up again. What we may miss, however, is that these exterior-focused changes don't always transform things. In these circumstances, we need to be looking elsewhere and recognise that the breakthrough we're looking for has to be an interior change.

A summary of key vertical development propositions

'Everything can be seen directly except... the eye through which we see' E.F. Schumacher, The Guide for the Perplexed. 1977.

- Horizontal learning at one's current stage is as important as vertical development towards the next. In fact, the optimal developmental strategy is a combination of both horizontal learning and vertical development.

- Our worldview and our filters, which includes our core beliefs, assumptions, attitudes and value judgements, acts as our frame of reference for interpreting the meaning of our experience. Some researchers believe that a person's frame of reference determines what they pay attention to and consider important, filtering everything else out.

- Most people have some awareness of their worldview but their filters are the eyes through which they see. This sets the purpose of vertical development which is to enable us to understand more about those filters which fundamentally shape how we make sense of the world. We may then choose to hold onto, let go or change them.

- The way in which we see more, and understand our filters, has been described by Kegan and Lahey as the Subject-Object shift described in detail in the previous chapter, 'Developmental frameworks and stage definitions – a map of the territory'. What was formerly in the unknown space (where we are subject to it) moves into the known space (where we can more objectively perceive it). Something comes out of the dark into the light and can be reflected upon.

- But this is more than reflecting on something new or a part of ourselves that has been previously repressed, disowned or buried. In Kegan's (1994) language, 'we have Object, we are Subject'. And once we have something, we are responsible, we have choices and decisions to make, we can act.

- The changing Subject-Object relationship defines developmental growth and propels stage change.

- According to Kegan, each of the stage changes – from socialised to self-authored to self-transforming – amounts to a fundamental restructuring of mind.

- With each fundamental shift that happens, the individual is more capable of dealing with complex environments and challenges. Research with organisational leaders suggests this significantly improves their effectiveness.

- When leaders struggle, or ultimately fail in their roles, the typical interpretation is the Peter Principle: that they've run out of capability. It's a competency issue. A vertical perspective would be that they've reached the limit of their development, not necessarily their capability. There is a mismatch between their level of development, and consciousness, and the complexities they're facing into.

- Complexity includes both outer dynamics such as the rapidly accelerating pace of change; and the inner dynamics of our personal lives.

- Kegan and Lahey described it as: "When we experience the world as 'too complex', we're not just experiencing the complexity of the world. We are experiencing a mismatch between the world's complexity and our own at this moment. There are only two logical ways to mend this mismatch – reduce the world's complexity or increase your own".

- Given the world's complexity isn't going to slow down, it's more likely to accelerate, we really only have one choice.

Vertical development applied to organisational leadership

- An individual's stage of development significantly affects how they understand their role, function and value in work and wider life, how they interact with others, and how they deal with adversity and complex issues. Indeed, it predicts how one even defines problems in the first place; for example, as a technical issue which has a specific solution if only we can find it, or as an adaptive challenge where the change is not in the outer game but in the inner game – within yourself.

- A number of research studies show that a very high proportion of managers and leaders (75-80%, depending on the study) are at diplomat, expert, and achiever stages of development. Refer to the previous chapter entitled Developmental frameworks and stage definitions – a map of the territory, for more detail.

- The achiever stage is the pinnacle of ordinary (conventional) adult development.

- In many ways, this is good news. To run any enterprise, you need experts and highly competent, results-focused, driven, achievement-oriented people. How else do you solve problems, get things done and achieve results?

- For many, the main currency at these stages is knowledge, information (data) and expertise. At expert and achiever, people tend to preference four things – knowing more, doing more, achieving more, and advancement. At the transition of expert/achiever, where a high percentage of managers and leaders profile, being busy, often overbusy, becomes a key feature of their lives. Action, at pace provides stimulation, excitement, challenge and huge satisfaction – especially when it's going well, their career progression timetable is on schedule, and the financial rewards are keeping up with expectation.

- Readers at these stages may recognise themselves in this description but rightly argue that it is partial and oversimplified. It should also be noted that, as people mature in these stages, they can also become highly reflective, curious, sensitive, interpersonally skilled, strategically aware, excellent leaders.

- For those people who transition to individualist, this picture starts to look different. What used to give them the buzz doesn't quite do it anymore. They can still perform the 'outer game of business' but it isn't everything anymore. New questions and concerns are emerging in their 'inner game'. Uncomfortable times can lie ahead as colleagues begin to pick up on their disquiet and question their commitment to the common purpose and collective core assumptions that we need all hands to the pumps and succeeding is everything. This can be tempered by what they also recognise as some valuable new perspectives, intelligent questions and useful critiquing. They may see this as thinking outside the box.

- Over-extended leaders caught up in the frenetic maelstrom don't always see the cost of the excessive hours and pressures on their energy, health, well-being and relationships. Many are living with high levels of exhaustion, stress, anxiety and pain. They don't know how to switch off. So, their periods of calm become increasingly rare. And for some, this only surfaces when they're already in an advanced stage of burnout or when their core relationships are in crisis. Perhaps, they've felt 'in over their heads' for some time but how do you say that to anyone when you don't even want to admit it to yourself.

- The accelerating pace of change and complexity is putting an evolutionary demand on leaders that we keep pace, or better still, more than match it by increasing our complexity of mind. This won't be achieved through more and more horizontal learning, even if it's from the very best academic institutes. Leaders also need to grow and develop vertically and recognise that inner, adaptive change will often be more important than outer, technical solutions.

- Without necessarily being conscious of it, leaders put in place organisational structures, practices, policies and cultures that emerge from their worldview (with all that is positive about that, and with all the limitations that go with any worldview). It has been argued that organisations cannot evolve beyond their leaderships' stage of development, Laloux (2014). There may be pockets of different ways of operating which reflect a different stage of consciousness, but in the main, the culture will be a reflection of the developmental stage of its senior leadership.

- This has led Anderson (2011) to conclude 'that there is no organisational transformation without a preceding transformation in the consciousness of the leadership'. His proposition is based on the idea that there is an inter-dependence between all levels of the system. The organisational system cannot organise at a higher stage of development than the leadership. And until the system organises at the new level of order, it hinders the development of most people in the system. Beyond that Anderson posits that 'only as the bulk of the population (of an organisation or society) develops to the new stage of development is there a possibility for the system to take its next evolutionary leap.'

- Laloux in his book 'Reinventing Organisations' was one of the first to apply stage development to organisations but is careful to stress that speaking of organisations as red, orange, green or teal, refers to their structures, practices, policies and cultures; not the stage development of their people nor the defining nature of social interaction. Clearly, in any sizeable organisation there will be a range of individual stages represented as the studies have shown. The highest proportion in most organisations will be in the conventional tier (diplomat, expert and achiever), with a far smaller number in preconventional (opportunist), and postconventional (individualist, strategist and alchemist).

- His focus on structures, practices and policies did however lead him to the conclusion that these do reveal the centre of gravity that pervades the 'main' organisational culture. Teams or divisions within large organisations operating at a higher centre of gravity are usually the product of local leadership, greater scope for autonomy and intentionally developmental team cultures.

- As leaders develop vertically, their perspective on what it really takes to transform their organisations evolves to a more sophisticated level. They understand the role of leadership differently and they see their people differently. The old technical paradigm shifts and they begin to appreciate what adaptive change really means, and as result of that, they come to a new appreciation that change really must start with them. This typically leads to a commitment to more empowered leadership styles, a coaching culture, an appreciation of multiple perspectives and the need to grow the capacity for collaboration. It becomes obvious that none of these can happen without higher levels of psychological mindedness and emotional intelligence both at the senior leadership level and throughout the organisation. In turn it requires a commitment to vertical growth and development.

- When there is the presence of later stage development leaders, and they set out to create more progressive organizational cultures, these contexts can pull people up and they can achieve outcomes they would not have thought possible. These more developmentally oriented cultures become very special places to work because there is a sense that everyone is growing and succeeding together. These can be the circumstances where genuine organisational transformation mirrors a multitude of personal transformations.

- For some people, it will only be these kinds of organisations, with a more conscious leadership, that will appeal to them. They will search out these beacon organisations but may still exit them if they don't find a culture that matches and keeps pace with their own desires to grow and develop.

- Research findings suggest that later stage, postconventional leaders – strategist and beyond - are more successful at leading organisational transformations. They have a greater capacity to deal with complexity, a higher psychological understanding of people, heightened emotional intelligence and a deeper appreciation of cultural dynamics. They are more welcoming of diverse ideas and perspectives, and can see more patterns and inter-connections. They not only see the dots but can join them up. And this in turn can lead to more creative solutions.

- However, the studies indicate that there are only around 8% of leaders at these stages of evolutionary growth at present and many executive teams don't possess any. This is sometimes mitigated by the presence of a later stage consultant or coach who has the ear of the CEO and the team.

- In an ever more challenging world this has brought many developmentalists to a similar conclusion. That the most significant priority in the leadership development space today is to find ways of accelerating the journey from the achiever to strategist stage of development. In his paper, Organisational Transformation requires the presence of leaders who are Strategists and Alchemists, Rooke (2001), states; 'my proposition is that only managers at the postconventional stages, Individualist and later, can steer transformational culture change. Managers at earlier stages would either not see the need or seeing it, would not have the inclusive frame-making ability to realise it. Even at the Individualist stage, the differentiated ability in transformational meaning-making and action is limited. Only at the Strategist stage does this capacity emerge with any possibility of consistency.'

- When we consider the implications of this proposition beyond the realm of business leadership and apply it to the political, social, economic and ecological challenges facing the world, it's full significance becomes ever more obvious.

To date, much of the literature on vertical development has focused on what vertical development is and why it's important. Developmental researchers and practitioners have set an important agenda. In section 2 – Vertical development – the how – I address the key questions of how vertical development happens, and what we know about how to accelerate its rate of progress.

Further reading and resources

Cook-Greuter, S.R. (2004). Making the case for a developmental perspective. Industrial and commercial training, 36(7), pp.275-281.

Cook-Greuter, S. (2013). Nine levels of increasing embrace in ego development: A full-spectrum theory of vertical growth and meaning making.

Cowan, C. and Beck, D. (1996). Spiral Dynamics: Mastering Values. Leadership and Change. Blackwell Publishers.

Gallwey, T. (2000). The Inner Game of Work. Random House.

Garvey-Berger, J. (2012). Changing on the job. Stanford Business Books.

Hayton, P. (2018). Understanding achiever consolidation and transition. Harthill Consulting, Unpublished paper.

Kegan, R. (1994). In over our heads: the mental demands of modern life. Harvard University Press.

Kegan, R. and Lahey, L. (2009). Immunity to change. Harvard Business Review Press, Boston, MA.

Kegan, R. and Lahey, L.L. (2016). An everyone culture: Becoming a deliberately developmental organization. Harvard Business Review Press.

Joiner, W.B. and Josephs, S.A. (2007). Leadership agility: Five levels of mastery for anticipating and initiating change. John Wiley & Sons.

Laloux, F. (2014). Reinventing Organisations. Nelson Parker.

Petrie, N. (2013). Vertical Leadership Development – Part 1 Developing Leaders for a Complex World. Center for Creative Leadership.

Rooke, D. and Torbert, W.R. (2005). Seven transformations of leadership. Harvard Business Review, 83(4), pp.66-76.

Rooke, D. (1997). Organisational transformation requires the presence of leaders who are strategists and magicians. Organisations and people, 4(3), pp.16-23.

Torbert, W.R., & Associates (2004). Action inquiry: The secret of timely and transforming leadership. Berrett-Koehler Publishers.

Watkins, A. & Wilbur, K. (2015). Wicked and Wise. Urbane Publications.

Watkins, A. (2015). 4D Leadership: Competitive Advantage Through Vertical Leadership Development. Kogan Page Publishers.

Wilber K. et al (2008). Integral Life Practice. Integral Books.

About the author

The founder of Courage and Spark©, practice leaders in the vertical development field, Peter Bluckert has created and led four international organisation development consultancies. During a consultancy and coaching career spanning nearly forty years, working with executives and teams from a wide range of private and public-sector organisations, Peter has built a reputation as both a thought-leader and innovative designer of transformational learning experiences. His desire to see improved standards in the field of Executive Coaching led him to join forces with other coaching pioneers and co-found the European Mentoring and Coaching Council (EMCC) in 2000 and he remains committed to this work.

Best described as a Practitioner, rather than Academic, he believes that good theory strengthens good practice and has published two coaching books (Psychological Dimensions of Executive Coaching and Right Here Right Now: Gestalt Coaching) and several journal articles. He is currently completing a new book on the Gestalt approach to vertical growth and development.

Peter is regularly asked to speak at International Conferences and has delivered presentations and programmes in Europe, the US, Asia, The Pacific and Africa.

Please feel free to get in touch.

grow@peterbluckert.com • www.peterbluckert.com

About Courage and Spark®

I want to briefly introduce you to Courage and Spark©. Firstly, why the choice and combination of words here? You probably already have a feel for it. The nature of 'inner-work', deeper self-exploration, is of itself a courageous act. Many people avoid it if they can, and only do it if their lives get too hot to handle. Spark? Because when people really re-connect to themselves, almost like coming back to themselves; when they get unstuck; and when they get in touch with their purpose and vision, there is a release of energy. You can often see the moment when the spark occurs. Re-ignition. A re-awakening and a renewed appetite for life.

Since establishing the company in 2010 my team and I have been privileged to deliver our vertical leadership programme to managers and leaders in a wide range of companies and on three continents. There have been a lot of sparks with a lot of courageous people and we've been delighted by the way it's been received.

In addition to our Courage and Spark© signature vertical leadership development programme, we offer a wider range of learning experiences to help people grow vertically. These include:

- A one-day route-mapping workshop to explain vertical development, and act as guide to how the journey can unfold.

- Vertical development coaching – both at the individual and team levels.

- Practitioner development for coaches and consultants in the Gestalt Approach to Vertical Growth and Development.

- A Knowledge Centre about the 'how' of vertical growth and development – including our books, white papers, articles and podcasts.

Please feel free to get in touch.

grow@courageandspark.com • www.courageandspark.com

Also in the 'Expand the Possible' series:

If this short book has grabbed your interest and you want to take it forward you may wish to know that this is part of a series of 'Expand the Possible' books covering vertical growth and development. Other books in the series include:

- **A comprehensive guide to vertical development**

- **Vertical development in the workplace**

- **Vertical development coaching: A Gestalt-Based Practitioner's Guide**

- **Vertical development: How it happens and how to accelerate it**

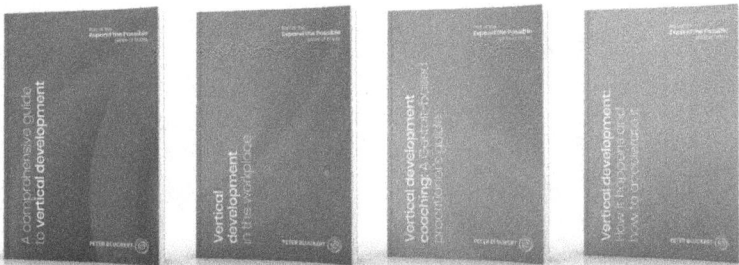

You may also be interested in two previously published books by Peter Bluckert:

www.ingramcontent.com/pod-product-compliance
Lightning Source LLC
Chambersburg PA
CBHW051040030426
42336CB00015B/2965